A Drop In The Bucket

_____
Name

_____
Date

Wine to Water Project

_____
Location

A Drop In The Bucket is your personal workbook. Here you will transfer your thoughts, feelings, ideas, prayers and dreams into words.

A Drop In The Bucket
Copyright © 2015

All Rights Reserved.
No part of this book may be reproduced in any form without permission in writing from the author or publisher.

All scripture verses are from The ESV® Bible (The Holy Bible, English Standard Version®) copyright © 2001 by Crossway, a publishing ministry of Good News Publishers, unless otherwise noted, and has been reproduced in cooperation with and by permission of Good News Publishers. All rights reserved.

ISBN: 978-1-935256-54-0

Ledge Press
PO Box 1652
Boone, NC 28607
ledgepress@gmail.com

Hello!

We are excited that you have chosen to serve with Wine To Water as an international volunteer! This is going to be a great experience with much learning and adventure around every corner. If you're reading this, you have already completed most, if not all, of the pre-trip requirements, so congratulations! Now, it's time to start preparing for your journey.

The purpose of a service trip is to give volunteers an opportunity to participate in one piece of the long-term process of learning about the water crisis, engaging with the culture, and serving in community around the world. Although this experience will be fun, Wine To Water service trips are NOT a vacation. We expect you to come ready to serve, get your hands dirty, and work hard for the duration of the trip. Your tasks will include community development and water projects, and you will be working directly with our ground partners throughout your service experience. It's important to keep in mind that you are not a superhero flying into these villages to save lives. But, by working alongside locals and helping maintain partnerships, you will be able to provide sustainable clean water and educational resources to those in need.

As an international traveler, there is a lot to consider before boarding your flight. The first thing to keep in mind is that you are about to enter into a completely different culture than what you are used to.

Different doesn't mean bad or wrong, it simply means different. You will experience different languages, different foods, different environments and different customs. It's important to remember that you're a visitor. We ask that you be flexible, maintain a positive attitude as you experience new things, and keep an open mind. Many times the hosts and nationals will do things differently than Westerners and it's important to submit to their leadership, even if you do not fully understand the reasoning behind it.

This Workbook is a resource for you to use, so that your thoughts, feelings, and experiences turn into documented words throughout the trip. I hope it will help your trip become an unforgettable experience that motivates you to continue serving in community.

I am so excited that you have decided to join us in the field. Your trip is going to be a fun, action-packed, humbling adventure. I hope that this Workbook is a helpful tool for you to use now, during your trip, and even after you return home.

Thank you for being willing to serve, for getting out of your comfort zone, for raising money to provide clean water around the world, and for caring enough to come help us. Welcome to the Wine To Water community!

Cheers,
Lisa Merritt
Director of Volunteer Programs

Our Mission

Wine To Water is committed to serving in community to provide clean water to those in need.

About Wine To Water
Wine To Water's US staff, although small in number, shares a huge passion for bringing clean water to folks in need. Our passion unites us and brings us joy as we work with our local partners on the ground. Wine To Water has worked in twenty-four countries, twelve of which are ongoing projects. We find it a privilege to support more than thirty international aid workers on four continents as we all work hard to fight this epidemic together.

What We Do
Each project is unique, but the common theme is that we partner with local people in each country. We develop leaders in the community and educate them on proper water and sanitation methods to promote sustainability. Our work empowers the local community to help them meet their ongoing needs.

How We Began
Doc Hendley is the founder and international president of Wine To Water. In 2003 he dreamed up the concept of the organization while bartending and playing music in nightclubs around Raleigh, North Carolina. The first fundraiser was held in January of 2004 and by August of that year, Doc was living in Darfur, Sudan installing

water systems for victims of the government-supported genocide. When Doc returned home in August of 2005, the haunting memories of what he had seen in Darfur drove him to continue building the organization he had started two years earlier.

In 2007, Wine To Water became an official 501(c)3 nonprofit. In 2009, Doc and the work of the Wine To Water team was recognized by the CNN Heroes program, launching the organization's efforts globally. Doc's dream, and the goal of Wine To Water, is to quench the thirst of those in need.

With every project, the common thread in our work is insuring that the proper type of water system is used for each specific community. Our methods include shallow and deep wells, well repairs, ceramic water filters, biosand filters, Sawyer PointONE filters, and rainwater harvest tanks. We also improve sanitation using latrine and hygiene education. We use local materials whenever possible. We monitor and report on all of our projects. We are constantly developing our programs and striving for more efficient systems.

Where We Work
Wine To Water has supported water projects in 24 countries: Belize, Dominican Republic, Costa Rica, Cambodia, Colombia, Brazil, Ecuador, Ethiopia, Guatemala, Haiti, Honduras, India, Kenya, Nepal, Peru, Philippines, South Africa, Sri Lanka, Sudan, Syria, Uganda, United States, Vietnam, Zimbabwe.

There are three stages to this journal, which reflect the three stages of your upcoming adventure.

The first stage is Preparation or **Pre-Trip**. During this stage you will be meeting with your team and preparing for the volunteer experience. You will be learning about the country and the people you will be serving. A few days prior to the launch of the trip, pull out your workbook. Listen. Read. Think. Pray. Record.

The second stage is **On the Ground**. It launches when your feet touch the ground in your host country. This will be an exciting and busy time. You will be "crowded" and your daily schedule filled with new experiences. You will have to be intentional in finding a time to slip away and be alone. During this time: Listen. Read. Think. Pray. Record.

The third stage is the **Post-Trip**. It begins when your feet touch the ground back in your home country. You will be enthusiastic about what you have just experienced and will want others to understand what you just went through, but they aren't able to. As you reflect on the memories of your trip, and sift through these conflicting emotions, you will begin to merge your recent adventure with the normal routines of being home and will eventually return to your normal routine. This is a critical time to capture what is passing through your mind and heart. During this stage: Listen. Read. Think. Pray. Record.

Pre-Trip Questions

1. What motivated you to participate in this trip?

2. What are you hoping to do, see, feel, accomplish on this trip?

3. What would you like to personally accomplish on this trip?

4. How can you prepare for this trip?

   Mentally?

   Physically?

   Spiritually?

5. Define the following concepts:

   Being Teachable

   Being Respectful

   Being Flexible

6. When you see a foreigner in your country, what do you expect from them? (Cultural norms? Language fluency? Ability to drive?)

7. How do you treat and/or view someone who is a foreigner in your country, city, and/or environment?

8. How do you hope you are treated by the locals as you enter into their world as a foreigner?

Daily Reflection: At the end of each day reflect on the following questions. As you reflect, jot down words that describe your day.

High—What was the highlight of your day? What was the most exciting, interesting, or energizing moment?

Low—What was the hardest part of your day? What was the most saddening, confusing, or frustrating moment for you?

Impact Image for the day. What image sticks out in your mind that made you realize the realities of where you are?

On the Ground

Day 1: Travel Day

Anyone who doesn't take truth seriously in small matters cannot be trusted in large ones either. — Albert Einstein

Walk with the wise and become wise, for a companion of fools suffers harm. Proverbs 13:20

1. What are you thinking? Feeling? Hoping?

2. Now that you are with your whole team in the field, what do you anticipate "serving in community" looking like?

Record your observations. What is going on around you?

Day 2: Orientation

The value of a man should be seen in what he gives and not in what he is able to receive. — Albert Einstein

So in everything, do to others what you would have them do to you, for this sums up the Law and the Prophets. Matthew 7:12

1. What is the purpose of the Volunteer Program at Wine To Water?

2. What is your purpose for this trip?

3. What are your first impressions of the

    Culture?

    People?

    Food?

    Community?

4. What does this statement mean?
   Don't prioritize your needs or desires at the expense of someone else's dignity.

5. What does it mean to be a team player?

Day 3: The Contract

Alone we can do so little; together we can do so much.
— Helen Keller

A new commandment I give to you, that you love one another: just as I have loved you, you also are to love one another. By this all people will know that you are my disciples, if you have love for one another. John 13:34-35

High

Low

Impact Image

The Contract:
- Be Here Now
- Give 110%
- Challenge by Choice
- Choose Joy
- Love Covers All

What are your personal goals for this trip?

Two years from now, what are two things in your life and actions that you would like to be different as a result of this trip?

Day 4

It ain't those parts of the Bible that I can't understand that bother me, it is the parts that I do understand.
— Mark Twain

Jesus answered, I am the way and the truth and the life.
John 14:6

High

Low

Impact Image

1. What are the five words or phrases that come to your mind when you think of poverty?

2. How a person defines poverty is often related to how they believe it should be alleviated. For example:

    - If you think poverty is a lack of knowledge, you may want to help educate the poor.
    - If you think poverty is oppression by powerful people, you may want to work for social justice.
    - If you think poverty is caused by personal sins or poor choices, you may want to evangelize and disciple the poor.
    - If you think poverty is a lack of material resources, you may want to contribute money or goods to poor communities.

3. How do you define poverty? How would you go about alleviating it?

4. How do you think an impoverished person defines poverty?

Stats: 2015 estimated: $2 billion is a conservative estimate of international service trips each year, which is also the equivalent of how much North Americans spend on flowers for Valentine's Day each year.

5. How much did your trip cost you? How much did it cost for the whole team? What does that amount equate to in the field?

6. Would you rather receive this amount of money or a team of volunteers for a week? How would our ground partners answer this question?

7. Is it worth it?

Day 5

I like your Christ, I do not like your Christians. Your Christians are so unlike your Christ. — Mahatma Gandhi

So we have stopped evaluating others from a human point of view. At one time we thought of Christ merely from a human point of view. How differently we know him now! This means that anyone who belongs to Christ has become a new person. The old life is gone; a new life has begun! And all of this is a gift from God, who brought us back to himself through Christ. 2 Corinthians 5:16-18, NLT

High

Low

Impact Image

1. Who are the poor? In what ways is this community rich? Poor? In what ways are we rich? Poor?

2. Helping or Hurting?

David Livermore, who has spent years studying cross-cultural engagement and short-term missions, shares a story that illustrates this dynamic. He and his wife, Linda, and their daughters were visiting Malaysia. After seeing a materially poor Malay father and daughter on the street, Livermore encouraged his own daughter to give the little girl a frog stuffed animal. "As we started to leave, the Malay father ordered his daughter to return the frog. We motioned that we didn't want it back, but he insisted. He began to raise his voice and grabbed the frog and handed it to me. As I began to talk with Linda about it we thought back to our home in the Chicago area. Though a beautiful house, our home was one of the more modest homes in our town. Linda asked, "So how would you feel if one of the parents in the million-dollar homes near us suddenly walked up to our girls and started handing them gifts?" All of a sudden I began to see this in a new light. I thought about how I would feel if some rich person started giving my girls unsolicited gifts in my presence. I'm quite capable of caring for them, thank you!" — Helping Without Hurting

3. Have you ever experienced this dynamic?

4. What are some ways you can engage with a community in true humility?

5. Is it easier or harder to work together as a team?

Day 6

You must be the change you wish to see in the world. — Mahatma Gandhi

And he said to them, "You shall love the Lord your God with all your heart, and with all your soul, and with all your mind. This is the great and first commandment. And a second is like it, You shall love your neighbor as yourself. On these two commandments depend all the Law and the Prophets." Matthew 22:37-40

High

Low

Impact Image

1. When is it okay to give something to someone?

2. Think about the community here. Is the current need mostly for relief, rehabilitation, or development?

RELIEF, REHABILITATION, AND DEVELOPMENT

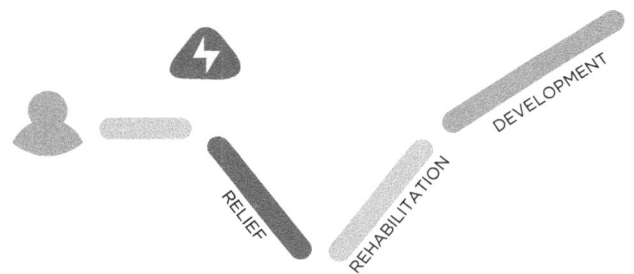

Relief—An effort to "stop the bleeding." It is the urgent and temporary provisions of emergency aid to reduce suffering from a natural or man-made crisis and it primarily utilizes a provider-receiver dynamic.

Rehabilitation—An effort to restore people back to their pre-crisis state after the initial bleeding has stopped, while also laying the basis for future development. In rehabilitation, people begin to contribute to improving their situation.

Development—Walking with people across time in ways that move all the people involved—both the "helpers" and the "helped"—closer to being in a right relationship with

God, self, others, and the rest of creation than they were before. This involved people identifying their problems creating solutions, and implementing those solutions. Development is often referred to as "empowerment." It avoids "doing for" and focuses on "doing with."

3. How do you define the difference between needs-based development and asset-based development?

4. Define paternalism.

5. What do these words mean:
   Family? Community? Team?

Day 7

When I admire the wonders of a sunset or the beauty of the moon, my soul expands in the worship of the creator.
— Mahatma Gandhi

The heavens declare to glory of God and the sky above proclaims his handiwork. Psalm 19:1

High

Low

Impact Image

1. How did you spend your time today? Who did you interact with today?

2. The trip is almost over. So, what do you want to challenge yourself to do tomorrow?

3. What is something you have learned from this community?

4. **People > Projects:** What does this mean?

5. What are you learning about being a part of a team/community and working together?

Day 8

If we are to go forward, we must go back and rediscover those precious values—that all reality hinges on moral foundations and that all reality has spiritual control. — Martin Luther King, Jr.

Trust in the Lord with all your heart and lean not on your own understanding; in all your ways acknowledge him, and he will make straight your paths. Proverbs 3:5-6

High

Low

Impact Image

1. How are you living out the contract (from Day 3 page 18)?

2. What are some ways you can continue the process of learning and engagement when you return home? For example, how can you:

    - Continue to support the work you are doing here?

    - Effectively alleviate poverty in your own community?

Write down some ideas about where to begin. It might be people, places, organizations, churches, or other ideas.

3. Revisit your goals from the beginning of the week. Have these goals changed? If so, what are your new goals?

Day 9: Reorientation

The pursuit of truth and beauty is a sphere of activity in which we are permitted to remain children all of our lives.
— Albert Einstein

Let the children come to me, do not hinder them, for to such belongs the kingdom of God. Mark 10:14

1. Write down two moments from your trip that had the most impact on you.

2. What was the most difficult part of the trip? What was the most saddening, confusing, or frustrating moment for you?

3. Think back to your first day. Have your first impressions changed?

   About team members?

   About the community?

   About the ground partners?

4. Which part of the service trip is the most important? Why? (Pre-trip? In the Field? Post-trip?)

5. Mosaic Image

6. How are you going to answer the question, "How was your trip?"

7. Was there a specific time during your trip that you felt your group become a team? Describe that moment.

8. John 6. Jesus feeds 5,000 people

9. What is one practical/tangible/measurable thing that you are going to do or change when you get back home?

10. Jot down answers to the below questions, then use these ideas to write a letter to yourself.

   What was your purpose for this trip?

   What did you learn from this community?

   How will you put what you learned into action when you get home? What is one thing you want to do or change when you get home?

As we re-enter your normal world there are five phases of emotional adjustment that are common after an international experience. Use these stages and reflect upon them during the following days and weeks.

Possible Stages for Re-entry
The following stages mention the cycle you may go through emotionally as you re-enter your home world.

Have **Fun** (honeymoon). Sharing the stories. Re-living the adventure.

Flee (avoidance). May begin to feel alone. Most of your family and friends have not had this adventure and cannot relate to what you have gone through and what you are feeling.

Fight (anger, criticism). Emotionally begin to fight back. Feelings of how unfair our way of life is compare to what you have just experienced. Anger at others not understanding.

Fit In (tolerance of differences). Survival. Acceptance and willing to acknowledge that others cannot know and experience what you feel. And acceptance of the idea that only when you experience something first-hand will understanding surface of what goes on in third world countries.

Forget. If you do not intentionally choose to go home and bear fruit, you will, by default, choose to forget.

OR

Be **Fruitful** (creative engagement). Finding ways to encourage others to share this same adventure you have had. Educating others and challenging others on the needs of the world, both spiritual needs and physical needs.

(Adapted from Lisa Espineli Chinn, Reentry Guide for Short Term Mission Leaders, *Orlando: DeeperRoots Publications p. 14, used by permission of the author.)*

Day 10: Travel Home

The best way to cheer yourself up is to try to cheer somebody else up. — Mark Twain

The generous will themselves be blessed, for they share food with the poor. Proverbs 22:9

1. What are you looking forward to the most?

2. How are you going to answer the question, "How was your trip?" when you get home?

3. What are some of your fears as you go home?

4. Write down what you are

   Feeling?

   Thinking?

   Hoping?

Post-Trip

I am only one, but still I am one. I cannot do everything, but still I can something; and because I cannot do everything, I will not refuse to do something I can do. — Helen Keller

And Jesus grew in wisdom and stature, and in favor with God and man. Luke 2:52

1. In what ways did the national hosts serve you and your team while you were on the ground? How does this relate to your culture back home?

2. How did your visit lead to positive change in a materially poor community?

3. What are your commitments? Write down what you want to do in the next..

   Two months

   Six months

   Year

4. Review your goals from Day 3 on page 15. Are you still working on achieving those goals?

5. What are some obstacles preventing you from reaching your goals?

6. How will you overcome these obstacles?

7. What have you done to report back to those who supported and sent you?

8. How can you stay connected and involved with Wine to Water?

Now that you have made Wine To Water a part of your personal story, there are many different ways to stay engaged with the community.

First, follow us on all of our different social channels, Facebook, Instagram, Twitter and read the **Cana** (medium.com/the-cana). This isn't just about staying up to date with the latest news, this is how you communicate with everyone in the Wine To Water community. Reach out to those living and working in countries around the world, stay in touch with other volunteers, let us know what you want to know more about and where you want to go next!

Second, order some **wine** and share it with friends and family! This could be a wonderful chance to share some of your experiences from your trip. Or give a bottle as a gift to someone special. You can order wine online at: winetowater.org/wine

Third, consider starting a **campaign** in your area, like an online fundraiser or an event, such as a wine tasting. We have plenty of information to help you get started and point you in the direction you would like to take your campaign. Check out our website on campaigns at: winetowater.org/campaigns

Fourth, find and join a local **chapter**! We have Wine To Water chapters in cities across the country. Chapters work together as a local community to organize events, spread the word about Wine To Water and plan for upcoming volunteer trips. If you don't have a chapter in your area, consider starting one! winetowater.org/chapters

Fifth, if you work in the food & beverage industry, you may be interested in our **Just One Shift** fundraising campaign during the week of World Water Day, March 22nd. For this campaign, bartenders, servers, restaurants and bars pledge to share their earnings from one shift to help solve the water crisis. If you don't work in the industry, find a local venue that is participating in Just One Shift and support them!

Last, but certainly not least, start thinking about your next **volunteer trip**! Keep an eye on our schedule and invite your friends and family to join you! winetowater.org/volunteer

Thank you for serving!
— WTW Team

Notes:

www.ingramcontent.com/pod-product-compliance
Lightning Source LLC
Chambersburg PA
CBHW070452050426
42450CB00012B/3245